CH. 242

54 - 145

# THE SOLAR SYSTEM

Chris Cooper

HODDER

*Wayland*

# ELECTRICITY AND MAGNETISM
# FORCES AND MOTION
# LIGHT AND SOUND
# THE SOLAR SYSTEM

Produced by Roger Coote Publishing
Gissing's Farm
Fressingfield
Suffolk
IP21 5SH

First published in Great Britain in 1999 by Macdonald Young Books

Reprinted in 2000 by Hodder Wayland,
an imprint of Hodder Children's Books

© Hodder Wayland 1999

Hodder Children's Books
A division of Hodder Headline Ltd
338 Euston Road
London NW1 3BH

**Design and typesetting** Victoria Webb
**Commissioning Editor** Lisa Edwards
**Editor** Roger Goddard-Coote
**Picture Researcher** Lynda Lines
**Illustrator** Alex Pang

Endpaper picture: The rings of the giant gas planet Saturn are a
swarm of millions of tiny moons, made of rock and ice.
Title page picture: The far side of the Moon

We are grateful to the following for permission to reproduce photographs:
Science Photo Library 12–13 (NOAO), 14 top (NASA), 14 centre (NASA), 17
(European Space Agency), 18 top (US Geological Survey), 19 bottom (NASA), 23
(NASA), 27 top (NASA), 29 (David A Hardy), 32 top (Detlev Van Ravenswaay), 32
bottom (François Gohier), 33 (Pekka Parviainen), 34 (European Space Agency).
Remaining photos are courtesy of Digital Vision.

The statistics given in this book are the most up to date available at
the time of going to press.

Printed in Hong Kong by Wing King Tong

A CIP catalogue record for this book is available from the British Library

ISBN 0 7500 2715 0

# CONTENTS

Words that are explained in the glossary are printed
in **bold** the first time they are mentioned in the text.

# INTRODUCTION

The solar system consists of the Sun and the many **planets** and other bodies that circle around it. These include the Earth and eight other planets, thousands of **comets** and **asteroids**, and countless millions of rocks and grains of dust. The first four planets, moving outwards from the Sun, are rocky and small – only a few thousands of kilometres across. The Earth is one of these. The next four planets are known as gas giants – globes of hydrogen, helium and other gases, tens of thousands of kilometres across. The outermost known planet, Pluto, is believed to be another rocky planet.

Though Pluto is the outermost of the known planets, it is not the farthest member of the solar system. The outer limit of the solar system is far beyond Pluto: an unseen cloud of 'sleeping comets', halfway between the Sun and the nearest **stars**.

The whole solar system belongs to an enormous system of stars, gas and dust called the Galaxy, which contains billions of stars. Circling many of these stars there must be other planetary systems like our own solar system.

## Gravitation

The solar system is held together by gravitation. This is a force with which every particle of matter in the universe pulls on every other particle. The Earth's gravitational pull keeps you held to the ground,

**Our Galaxy contains 100 billion stars, together with gas and dust, in a swirling spiral 100,000 light years across.**

and it holds artificial **satellites** and the Moon in their paths around the Earth. Because it contains so much matter, the Sun has a huge gravitational pull, which is strong enough to keep all the other members of the solar system from escaping into distant space.

All the planets except Mercury and Venus have natural satellites, or moons, circling around them. The moons are prevented from escaping by the planets' own gravitational pulls. The Earth has just one satellite – the Moon – but each of the gas giants has a family of them, like a miniature solar system.

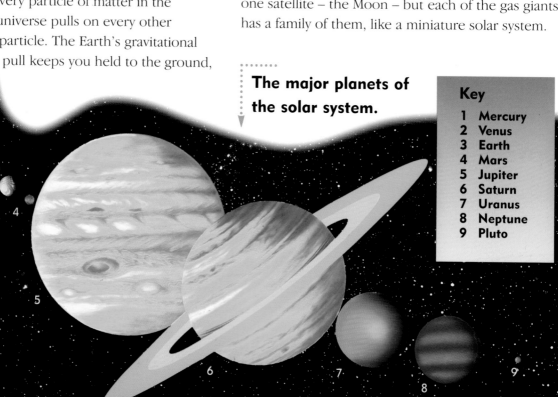

Sun

**The major planets of the solar system.**

| Key | |
|---|---|
| 1 | Mercury |
| 2 | Venus |
| 3 | Earth |
| 4 | Mars |
| 5 | Jupiter |
| 6 | Saturn |
| 7 | Uranus |
| 8 | Neptune |
| 9 | Pluto |

Key

| 1 | Mercury | 8 | Neptune |
| 2 | Venus | 9 | Pluto |
| 3 | Earth | 10 | Sun |
| 4 | Mars | 11 | Asteroids |
| 5 | Jupiter | 12 | Halley's Comet |
| 6 | Saturn | 13 | Comet Swift-Tuttle |
| 7 | Uranus | 14 | Kuiper Belt |

The paths of the planets and satellites are called **orbits**. They are **elliptical** (shaped like flattened circles). A planet travels fastest in the part of its orbit nearest to the Sun, slower farther out. The larger a planet's orbit, the longer it takes to travel around the Sun.

## Different Worlds

Humans have not yet landed on any other planet or satellite except the Moon. However, astronomers have found out a great deal about the planets from observations made with their telescopes and with unmanned space probes. They know that the planets of the solar system are very different from each other. For example, some are hotter than boiling water, while others are far colder than ice. In the future, as space travellers explore the solar system, we shall find out much more.

## FACT FILE

### SOLAR SYSTEM DATA

Diameter: 14,750 million kilometres
Distance from centre of Galaxy: 30,000 light years
Speed at which solar system moves
 around the centre of the Galaxy: 220 kilometres per second
Number of major planets: 9
Number of known planetary satellites: 64

Note: A light year is the distance light travels in 1 year; it is equal to 9.46 million million kilometres.

The top diagram shows the inner solar system, from the Sun out to the asteroid belt. The bottom diagram shows the outer solar system. The planets (except Pluto) and the asteroids move in almost the same plane, but the orbits of many comets are tilted.

# BIRTH OF THE SOLAR SYSTEM

**1. The solar system began to form about 4.5 billion years ago, when a huge, swirling cloud of gas and dust was pulled together by its own gravity.**

**2. The Sun began to glow in the centre of the cloud. Around it, 'knots' of denser gas and dust formed. They would eventually become the planets.**

Most astronomers believe that the solar system began 4.5 billion **years** ago, when a cloud of gas and dust, just one of many thousands in the Galaxy, began to shrink. It probably did so because it had been disturbed by the explosion of a nearby star. As the matter in the cloud crowded together, the gravitational attraction of each particle for every other particle became stronger. The gas and dust fell faster and faster towards the centre, and the cloud began to spin faster and faster. As particles rubbed against each other, the gas and dust heated up. The heat increased the **pressure** at the centre, which stopped the cloud from shrinking any more. As the temperature rose, nuclear reactions began in the heart of the cloud, turning hydrogen atoms into helium atoms. A new star had been born – the Sun.

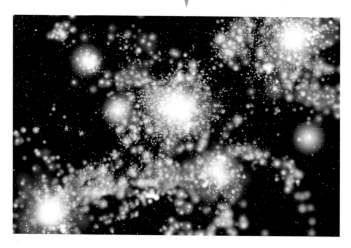

**In the Great Nebula in the constellation of Orion, new stars are being born. Some may have planets like those in the solar system.**

## The Planets Form

A strong solar 'wind' blew from the Sun, consisting of fragments of atoms, smashed by the intense heat. The **solar wind** and the intense sunlight blew away much of the gas from the central regions of the cloud. But grains of dust remained behind and collected together, pulled by their own gravitational attraction. Clumps of dust built up, collided to form larger clumps, attracted more dust by gravitation, and gradually built up into the rocky inner planets. This process may have taken about 100 million years.

In the cold, slow-moving gas and dust farther from the Sun, similar rocky bodies formed more quickly. The largest ones gathered huge **atmospheres** of hydrogen and helium around them. It took only about 10 million years for these giant planets to grow. Smaller bodies clustered around each one, forming their families of satellites.

## FUTURE FILE

### OTHER PLANETARY SYSTEMS

It is very likely that most stars are born with their own systems of planets. But such planets are so hard to see in even the most powerful telescopes because they are so far away. Only a few giant planets have been detected circling other stars.

Discs of dust, looking just as our solar system would have looked when it was only a few hundred million years old, have been discovered circling some nearby stars, such as the bright stars Vega and Fomalhaut. There are big holes in the middle of the discs, probably 'swept clean' by young orbiting planets that we are not able to detect.

## Left-over Matter

Some of the matter in the newly born solar system did not become part of the planets or satellites. It stayed independent, in the form of rocks and dust grains that pelted the planets for perhaps 600 million years. The bombardment gradually died away as the 'cosmic dust' was used up, but we can still see the evidence today in the scarred surfaces of some planets and moons.

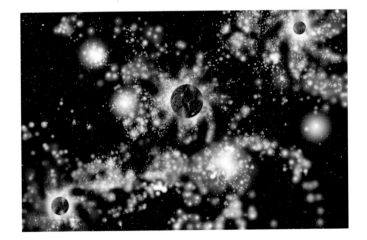

**3. Small, rocky planets formed in the warm inner regions near the Sun. Huge gas giants formed in the cold outer regions.**

**4. Today the planets get light and heat from the Sun, which should continue to burn steadily for another 5 billion years.**

# THE SUN

In a hydrogen bomb a few kilograms of hydrogen are turned into helium in a fraction of a second, releasing devastating quantities of energy. But in the Sun, 700 million tonnes of hydrogen are turned into helium every second. And this outpouring of energy has been going on at much the same rate for the last 5 billion years. But this enormous, long-lasting explosion is so far away that its heat and light do not destroy life on Earth – they make life possible.

## The Sun's Core

At the centre of the Sun the temperature is 15 million °C, which means that particles of matter move around at very high speeds. The pressure is 300 billion times the pressure of the Earth's atmosphere at sea level. In this environment atoms are broken down into pieces. The atom fragments are nuclei (the cores of the atoms) and electrons (which make up the outer parts). These fragments are constantly colliding with each other, and sometimes the hydrogen nuclei merge to form heavier nuclei. These also collide and from time to time merge. The final result of this sequence of reactions is to turn four nuclei of hydrogen into one nucleus of helium, while releasing energy that keeps the Sun hot.

**Energy travels from the centre of the Sun to its surface and travels into space as light, heat and other kinds of radiation.**

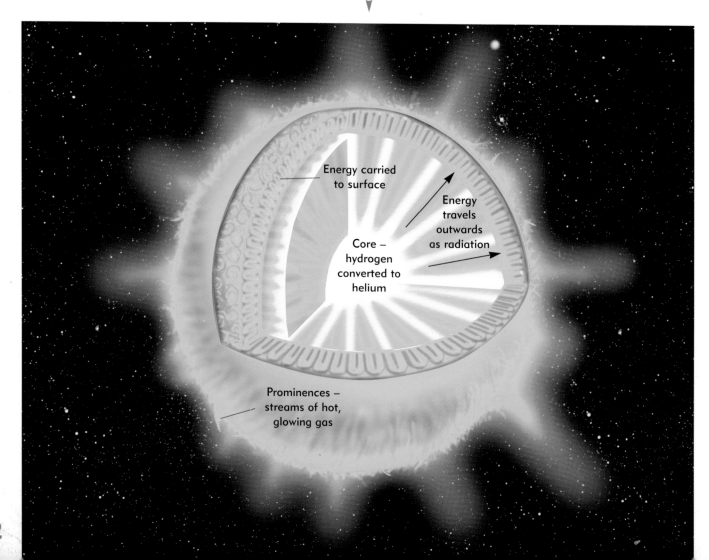

Energy carried to surface

Energy travels outwards as radiation

Core – hydrogen converted to helium

Prominences – streams of hot, glowing gas

**WARNING!**
Never look directly at the Sun, either with the naked eye or through a telescope or binoculars. You could damage your vision for life. Dark glass or plastic filters are not safe – they often let through damaging invisible rays.

**Sunspots appear as dark red patches in this picture of the Sun.**

## The Face of the Sun

The surface of the Sun seethes with violent activity. There are light and dark patches, hundreds or thousands of kilometres across, giving the surface a mottled appearance. ('Dark' here means less bright than the surroundings – all of the Sun's surface is blindingly bright.)

There are huge patches called sunspots, often bigger than the Earth. They are relatively cool holes in the surface where the Sun's intense magnetic field has broken through the surface from the interior and slows down the outward flow of heat. Sunspots build up in size and numbers, reaching a maximum every 11 years and then fading away again.

Astronomers can find out how fast the Sun rotates by measuring how long sunspots take to move across the visible face of the Sun, or to reappear after vanishing round its far side. They find that, because the Sun is gaseous and not solid, different parts turn at different rates. The Sun takes slightly less than 4 weeks to rotate at its equator, but over 5 weeks at its poles.

Sometimes explosions called flares are seen on the Sun. They last only minutes or hours, and pour out visible light, X-rays and other **radiation**. The particles travel across space, and those that reach the Earth can disturb radio communications and pose a danger to space travellers.

**An enormous arch of glowing hydrogen gas erupts from the Sun's surface.**

## FACT FILE

### SUN DATA

| | |
|---|---|
| Rotation period: | 26 days (equator); 37 days (poles) |
| Diameter at equator: | 1,392,000 km |
| Volume: | 1,304,000 (Earth = 1) |
| Mass: | 1.99 billion billion billion tonnes = 329,000 x mass of Earth |
| Temperature: | 5,500 °C (surface); approx. 15 million °C (centre) |
| Density: | 1.41 (water = 1) |

# MERCURY AND VENUS

Two planets lie closer to the Sun than the Earth does. One is Venus, which is almost the same size as the Earth, and covered in a thick atmosphere. Once it was thought that Venus was the planet most like the Earth, and that there might be oceans and even life beneath the clouds. The other planet is tiny Mercury, closest to the Sun of all the planets.

## The Swift Planet

Mercury's 'year' – the time it takes to orbit the Sun – is just 88 Earth **days**. Yet the time it takes to rotate once is nearly 2 months, compared with 24 hours for Earth. The result is that daylight and night-time on Mercury are each 88 days long.

Mercury's gravity is too weak to have held on to any atmosphere it may have had in the past. Its daytime side has no protection from the intense glare of the Sun, and the temperature can climb to over 420 °C – high

The rocky surface of Mercury is scarred by meteoric craters, most of them billions of years old.

Powerful winds circle the globe of Venus. The clouds consist of droplets of sulphuric acid.

## TEST FILE

### WATCHING MERCURY AND VENUS

Mercury and Venus appear in the western sky after sunset at certain times of the year (and in the eastern sky before sunrise at other times). This table gives the dates on which they appear highest in the west, up to the year 2005.

Warning: do not search for Mercury or Venus before the sun is below the horizon.

### Mercury

Mercury is visible for a few days before and after the dates shown here. It does not appear until about 40 minutes after sunset.

| | |
|---|---|
| 1999 | 3 March, 28 June, 24 October |
| 2000 | 14 February, 8 June, 6 October |
| 2001 | 29 January, 21 May, 19 September |
| 2002 | 12 January, 4 May, 31 August, 26 December |
| 2003 | 16 April, 14 August, 9 December |
| 2004 | 29 March, 26 July, 20 November |
| 2005 | 12 March, 8 July, 3 November |

### Venus

At its brightest, Venus looks brighter than any star. It appears in the evening sky every 19 months, but it is easily visible for at least 2 months before each of the dates given here. It is at its brightest 5 weeks after each date.

| | |
|---|---|
| 1999 | 11 June |
| 2000 | (not visible) |
| 2001 | 17 January |
| 2002 | 22 August |
| 2003 | (not visible) |
| 2004 | 29 March |
| 2005 | 3 November |

enough to melt lead. But at midnight, the temperature drops to below −180 °C.

The surface of Mercury looks much the same as our Moon's surface. It is peppered with craters made by a barrage of **meteoroids** when the solar system was young. In places there are rocky plains, where large impacts caused molten lava to flood from beneath the surface.

## The Hothouse Planet

Although Venus is farther from the Sun than Mercury, its surface is even hotter because the planet's heat is trapped by its dense atmosphere of carbon dioxide. Temperatures can reach 740 °C.

The atmospheric pressure at the surface is about 90 times the air pressure on the surface of the Earth. The few spacecraft that have landed on Venus have been crushed and roasted into silence after sending back data for only a few minutes.

Bright clouds made of droplets of sulphuric acid completely cover the planet, reflecting sunlight so strongly that Venus is the brightest object in our sky, apart from the Sun and Moon. Radar waves from orbiting spacecraft have penetrated the clouds to reveal mountains, craters, plains, and dead volcanoes. The Maxwell Mountains, for example, tower 17 kilometres high – nearly twice the height of Earth's Mount Everest.

**The high mountains and rocky plains of Venus, as shown by radar scanning.**

## FACT FILE

### MERCURY AND VENUS DATA

| Planet | Mercury | Venus |
|---|---|---|
| Distance from Sun (million km): | 57.9 | 108.2 |
| Year (Time to go round Sun): | 88.0 days | 224.7 days |
| Day (Time to revolve on axis): | 58 days 15 hours 30 mins | 243 days |
| Diameter at equator (km): | 4,878 | 12,104 |
| Known moons: | 0 | 0 |
| Mass (Earth=1): | 0.055 | 0.815 |
| Surface gravity (Earth=1): | 0.38 | 0.88 |

# EARTH

Planet Earth is only slightly bigger than Venus. The two planets have similar mass and gravity. Yet conditions on the surface are very different. The atmosphere is rich in nitrogen and oxygen, and contains very little carbon dioxide. Oceans cover 74 per cent of the surface. Living things flourish in the air and the oceans and on the land.

The Earth is farther from the Sun than Venus is, and its atmosphere contains much less carbon dioxide to trap the Sun's heat. As a result, the Earth is much cooler than Venus – the average temperature on the surface is about 15 °C.

## Inside the Earth

Radioactive elements in the Earth's rocks, mainly uranium and thorium, heat the inside of the Earth. The temperature at the centre of the Earth is at least 4,500 °C. Scientists believe that the core consists of iron and nickel. Its outer parts are liquid, but the central core is squeezed into a solid form by the pressure of the overlying matter.

Outside the core is the mantle, which consists of rock and makes up most of the Earth. Its upper layer, about 300 kilometres thick, is able to move, like a very thick, treacly liquid. The heat flowing from the interior makes it churn – rather as the heat from a gas flame makes the soup in a pot rise and fall, except that the churning of the outer mantle takes millions of years.

**The atmosphere and oceans form a thin skin over the Earth's surface. The planet's interior has a complicated structure, with a hot core.**

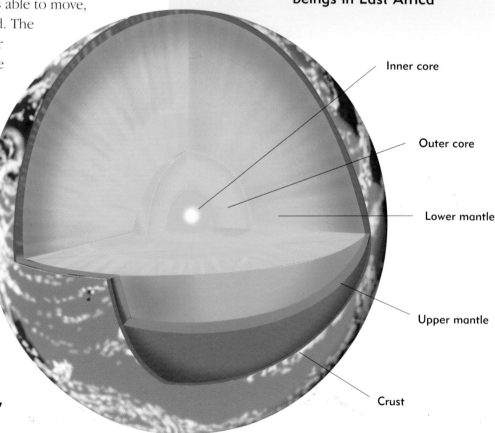

Inner core

Outer core

Lower mantle

Upper mantle

Crust

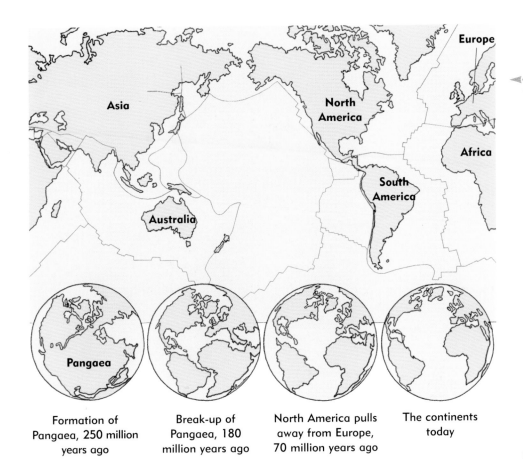

Asia

North America

Europe

Africa

South America

Australia

Pangaea

Formation of Pangaea, 250 million years ago

Break-up of Pangaea, 180 million years ago

North America pulls away from Europe, 70 million years ago

The continents today

**The continents ride on rigid areas of the crust, called plates (the boundaries between the plates are shown in red). Today's continents were formed over the last 180 million years by the break-up of a single supercontinent called Pangaea.**

**The Earth is the only planet that is rich in water and oxygen.**

## The Earth's Crust

The outermost layer of the Earth – the crust – consists of less dense rocks that literally float on the denser rock of the mantle. The crust is 5–10 kilometres thick beneath the oceans; the continents consist of crust 20–65 kilometres thick. The rocks of the crust are mostly made of silicon and metals such as aluminium and iron, combined with oxygen. Crustal rocks are moved about by the churning of the mantle rocks beneath. Over hundreds of millions of years continents are carried about and collide with each other.

## FACT FILE

### EARTH DATA

| | |
|---|---|
| Distance from Sun (million km): | 149.6 |
| Year (Time to go round Sun): | 365.26 d |
| Day (Time to revolve on axis): | 23 h 56 m |
| Diameter at Equator (km): | 12,756 |
| Known moons: | 1 |
| Mass (Earth=1): | 1 (= 5,980 billion billion tonnes) |
| Surface gravity (Earth=1): | 1 (= 9.81 metres per second per second) |

# MARS

**M**ars is called the Red Planet because its reddish colour is easily visible to the naked eye. It is red because its surface is a desert covered with sands made of compounds of iron and oxygen – similar to iron rust. The Martian atmosphere consists mostly of carbon dioxide. It is very thin, and its pressure at the surface is less than one hundredth of that at the Earth's surface. But winds on Mars are strong enough to raise sand storms that can hide the surface from view for weeks at a time.

## The Ice Caps

The Martian atmosphere is so thin because gravity is too weak to hold an atmosphere. Liquid water cannot exist – it would soon turn into vapour. Most of the tiny amount of water on Mars is frozen in the polar caps. The southern cap is permanently coated with frozen carbon dioxide. The northern polar cap is coated with carbon dioxide during the winter, but this evaporates during the summer.

**The giant volcano Mons Olympus towers 27 km above the Martian desert.**

**A huge system of canyons called Valles Marineris stretches for thousands of kilometres across Mars.**

## TEST FILE

### WATCHING MARS

Mars is at its brightest roughly every 2 years and 7 weeks. It is then at opposition – that is, opposite to the Sun as seen from Earth. It rises in the east as the Sun is setting in the west, and is high in the sky at midnight. These are the dates of opposition up to 2005, with the constellations where Mars can be found.

| | | |
|---|---|---|
| 1999 | 24 April | Virgo |
| 2001 | 13 June | Sagittarius |
| 2003 | 28 August | Capricornus |
| 2005 | 7 November | Aries |

Millions of years ago Mars had a thicker atmosphere. There was liquid water on the surface, perhaps released when vast quantities of underground ice were melted by volcanic eruptions. There were floods that carved valleys which still exist today. A network of valleys, called the Valles Marineris, dwarfs the Grand Canyon on Earth. The system is 4,000 kilometres long – long enough to stretch across the United States – and is 700 kilometres across at its widest part, and 7 kilometres deep.

## Tall Mountains, Deep Valleys

Heat from inside Mars built up huge volcanoes in the past, though they are all dead now. Mons Olympus is a volcano 27 kilometres high – the tallest mountain in the solar system. In the past, impacts with asteroids or comets have flung pieces of Martian rock into space, and some have been found on Earth as **meteorites**. There are also thousands of craters on Mars, partly worn down by millions of years of sand storms.

*Viking* space probes that landed on Mars in 1976 searched for signs of life in rocks, but found no definite evidence for it. But many scientists think there is a chance that simple forms of life exist near the polar caps or deep underground.

**The diameter of Mars is just over half that of the Earth.**

## FACT FILE

**MARS DATA**

| | |
|---|---|
| Distance from Sun (million km): | 227.9 |
| Year (Time to go round Sun): | 687.0 d |
| Day (Time to revolve on axis): | 24 h 37 m |
| Diameter at equator (km): | 6,794 |
| Known moons: | 2 |
| Mass (Earth=1): | 0.11 |
| Surface gravity (Earth=1): | 0.38 |

**Scattered rocks in the Martian desert in this photograph taken by a *Viking* robot spacecraft that landed in 1976.**

# ASTEROIDS

Thousands of tiny objects, called 'asteroids', 'planetoids', or 'minor planets', circle the Sun. Most move in orbits that lie between Mars and the next major planet, Jupiter. There is a large gap between these two planets, and in 1800 a group of astronomers got together to search for a faint planet moving in this region. They called themselves the 'Celestial Police'. But before they could start work, an Italian astronomer, Giuseppe Piazzi, found the first asteroid, later called Ceres. The Celestial Police began searching and in the following 6 years they found three more tiny asteroids – Pallas, Vesta and Juno.

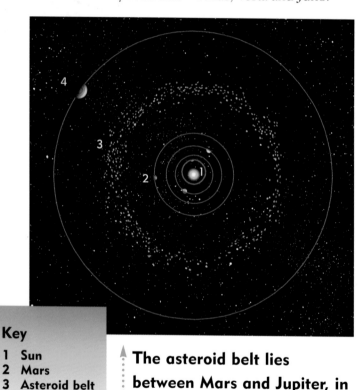

**Key**
1 Sun
2 Mars
3 Asteroid belt
4 Jupiter

▲ **The asteroid belt lies between Mars and Jupiter, in a gap in the planets' orbits.**

## Asteroids by the Thousand

The next asteroids were not found until 1845 and 1847. From then on, not a year passed without more asteroids being discovered. From 1891 photography was used to search for asteroids, and then many were discovered. But of all the asteroids, only Vesta is ever bright enough to be seen with the naked eye.

Once it was thought that asteroids were the pieces of a planet that had been destroyed in an explosion or a collision. Now it is thought that they

## TEST FILE

### THE TITIUS-BODE RULE
The Celestial Police were guided in their search for asteroids by a rule named after two German astronomers, Johann Daniel Titius and Johann Elert Bode. The Titius-Bode rule generates a series of numbers in this way: – Start with 0,3, and then keep doubling the numbers after that, to give:
0, 3, 6, 12, 24, 48, 96, 192, 384, 768

Add 4 to each number, to give:
4, 7, 10, 16, 28, 52, 100, 196, 388, 772

Then divide by 10, to give:
0.4, 0.7, 1.0, 1.6, 2.8, 5.2, 10.0, 19.6, 38.8, 77.2

Compare this series with the distances of the planets from the Sun (with the Earth–Sun distance taken as 1.0):

| Planet | True distance | Titius-Bode Rule distance |
| --- | --- | --- |
| Mercury | 0.4 | 0.4 |
| Venus | 0.7 | 0.7 |
| Earth | 1.0 | 1.0 |
| Mars | 1.5 | 1.6 |
| | | 2.8 |
| Jupiter | 5.2 | 5.2 |
| Saturn | 9.5 | 10.0 |
| Uranus | 19.2 | 19.6 |
| Neptune | 30.1 | 38.8 |
| Pluto | 39.4 | 77.2 |

The numbers give a good approximation to the distances of the planets as far as Uranus (then the farthest known planet), except that there is a gap at 2.8. In this gap the astronomers discovered the asteroids.

consist of matter that was never able to gather into a single body because of the effect of Jupiter's gravity.

However, some of the asteroids have collided with each other and broken up in the past. One, Psyche, is almost pure nickel-iron – the same

**The impact of an asteroid on the Earth would almost certainly mean the death of the entire human race.**

## FUTURE FILE

**WHAT IF AN ASTEROID HIT THE EARTH?**
If an asteroid 1 kilometre across hit the Earth, it would blast a big area and create huge waves in the oceans and the ground itself. A dust cloud would be formed that would last for years, cooling the whole Earth. Humans would probably not survive. Many scientists believe that an impact like this – or the vast amounts of dust it would have caused – wiped out the dinosaurs and thousands of other animal and plant species 65 million years ago.

is about a quarter of the distance to the Moon. The asteroid was only about 6–13 metres across, but that would have been big enough to do considerable damage if it had hit the Earth.

**The asteroid Vesta is so small that its gravity is not strong enough to pull it into a globular shape (see page 29).**

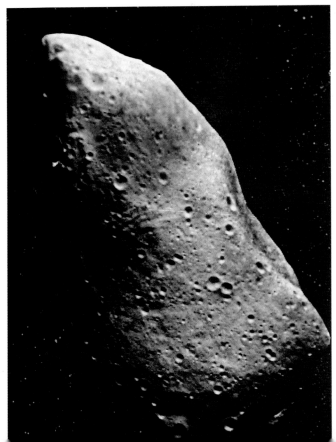

substance that the molten core of the Earth is made of. Psyche was probably once part of the core of a larger body.

### Small but Deadly

If all the asteroids, known and yet to be discovered, were put together, they would make only a tiny body, with a mass of about a thirtieth of the Moon's. The biggest, Ceres, accounts for nearly half the total mass of the asteroids.

Some asteroids move in orbits that take them far from the main belt between Mars and Jupiter. 'Earth-crossing' asteroids are those whose orbits cross the orbit of the Earth. Some come close to the Earth by astronomical standards. In 1994 an asteroid called $XM_1$ passed 104,000 kilometres from the Earth. That

# JUPITER

The giant planet Jupiter is as large as 1,300 Earths. The planet consists of a great ball of hydrogen and helium, with small amounts of other elements – a sample of the gases from which the whole solar system formed. We are able to see only the tops of the clouds of frozen ammonia crystals that cover the planet. The clouds form dark-coloured stripes called belts, and light ones called zones.

In the southern hemisphere is the Great Red Spot, a swirling storm that is broader than the Earth. The Great Red Spot was first observed in 1664 or 1665, when telescopes first became powerful enough to show it, and it shows no signs of dying away. There are smaller storms over the whole planet, and lightning flashes send out radio noise that can be detected on Earth.

**Jupiter, the largest planet in the solar system, is a globe of hydrogen, helium, and other gases over 1,300 times the size of the Earth.**

## TEST FILE

### WATCHING JUPITER
Jupiter is at its brightest when it is opposite in the sky to the Sun. It is then high in the sky at midnight. At its brightest, Jupiter appears brighter than any other planet except Venus. Here the dates of opposition are given to 2005, with the constellations in which Jupiter is found.

| 1999 | 23 October | Aries |
|------|------------|-------|
| 2000 | 28 November | Taurus |
| 2001 | (not at opposition) | |
| 2002 | 1 January | Gemini |
| 2003 | 2 February | Cancer |
| 2004 | 4 March | Leo |
| 2005 | 3 April | Virgo |

### The Structure of Jupiter
The gaseous part of Jupiter's atmosphere probably takes up the top 1,000 kilometres of the planet. The pressure towards the centre is enormous – enough to crush hydrogen gas into liquid form. Deeper down, the hydrogen is compressed into a hard, metal-like form. At the very centre of Jupiter there is probably a core of rock and iron. Jupiter gives out slightly more heat than it receives from the Sun, so its centre must be hot – at least 20,000 °C – far hotter than the surface of the Sun.

## FACT FILE

### JUPITER DATA

| | |
|---|---|
| Distance from Sun (million km): | 778 |
| Year (Time to go round Sun): | 11.9 y |
| Day (Time to revolve on axis): | 9 h 50 m |
| Diameter at equator (km): | 142,984 |
| Known moons: | 16 |
| Mass (Earth=1): | 317.8 |
| Surface gravity (Earth=1): | 2.6 |

**The Great Red Spot is a storm in Jupiter's atmosphere that has been raging for centuries.**

Gaseous hydrogen

Core of rock and iron

Solid hydrogen

Liquid hydrogen

**Inside Jupiter the huge pressure crushes the hydrogen gas into liquid and solid forms. There may be a small core of rock and iron.**

### Gravity on Jupiter

Jupiter has 318 times the mass of the Earth. It contains 70 per cent of the mass of all the objects in the solar system apart from the Sun. The visible surface is 11 times as far from the centre of Jupiter as the Earth's surface is from our planet's centre. So despite the planet's huge mass, the force of gravity at the surface is only 2.6 times that on the Earth. Jupiter rotates in less than 10 hours – so fast that the atmosphere is thrown outwards strongly at the equator. Through a telescope, the planet can clearly be seen to be elliptical.

# SATURN

Among the planets Saturn is second only to Jupiter in size. It circles the Sun 9.5 times as far from the Sun as the Earth does. It is cold and dark this far from the Sun: Saturn receives less than one ninetieth as much light and heat as the Earth. But the planet is girdled by spectacular broad, flat rings, more impressive than any others in the solar system.

## Saturn's Rings

The rings are made of millions of small chunks of matter, each following its own orbit around the planet. The chunks are made of ordinary water ice or of rock coated with ice. No one knows whether the rings were formed at the same time as Saturn, or were produced later by the collision of two small satellites or asteroids.

Through Earth-based telescopes, the rings look flat and featureless, apart from several gaps. But the *Voyager 1* spacecraft, which visited Saturn in 1980, discovered that they are made up of at least 10,000 thin individual rings called 'ringlets'.

## TEST FILE

### WATCHING SATURN
Saturn is at its brightest every year and 13 days, looking like a bright yellowish 'star'. The rings are edge-on to us roughly every 15 years and very hard to see. But throughout the period covered by this table they will be a fine sight in small telescopes or binoculars, and in 2002 they will appear fully 'opened out'. The dates are given below, with the constellation in which Saturn appears.

| | | |
|---|---|---|
| 1999 | 6 November | Aries |
| 2000 | 19 November | Taurus |
| 2001 | 4 December | Taurus |
| 2002 | 17 December | Taurus |
| 2003 | 31 December | Gemini |
| 2004 | (not at its brightest) | |
| 2005 | 13 January | Gemini |

**This diagram shows how our view of Saturn's rings changes.**

1980
1983
1986
1989
1992
1995

**Some of the thousands of 'ringlets' that make up the rings of Saturn. This picture was taken by the *Voyager 2* spacecraft.**

The gaps in the rings are caused by the gravity of Saturn's inner satellites. The tiny satellite Pan actually moves inside a gap called Encke's Division. The most sharply defined gap, called Cassini's Division, is caused by Mimas and Enceladus, which lie well beyond the rings. Other satellites affect the ringlets, giving some of them a kinked or braided appearance.

# FACT FILE

## SATURN DATA
| | |
|---|---|
| Distance from Sun (million km): | 1,427 |
| Year (Time to go round Sun): | 29.5 y |
| Day (Time to revolve on axis): | 10 h 14 m |
| Diameter at equator (km): | 120,536 |
| Known moons: | 19 |
| Mass (Earth=1): | 95.1 |
| Surface gravity (Earth=1): | 1.15 |

## The Globe of Saturn
Like Jupiter, Saturn is made up mostly of hydrogen, with some helium and traces of other substances. At the centre is a solid, rocky core, at a temperature of at least 15,000 °C. Outside this the hydrogen is crushed into a hard, metal-like state by the pressure. Above this, extending perhaps half-way to the surface, the hydrogen is liquid. Outside this liquid layer is the gaseous hydrogen atmosphere. The cloud-tops are not as strongly marked as those on Jupiter, but brown and white spots and cloud belts have been observed by spacecraft and Earth-based telescopes.

**The globe of Saturn is flattened at the top and bottom.**

1997

2000

2003

2006

2009

# FUTURE FILE

## THE CASSINI MISSION
In October 1997 the *Cassini* spacecraft was launched from Cape Canaveral on a 7-year journey to Saturn. The survey of Saturn and its moons following its arrival in July 2004 is designed to last at least 4 years. *Cassini* carried a probe called *Huygens*, designed to parachute on to Saturn's moon Titan and make observations of its surface and atmosphere.

# URANUS AND NEPTUNE

Far beyond Saturn, the third of the gas giants, Uranus, moves around the Sun. It takes over 84 Earth years to complete one orbit. Uranus is just visible to the naked eye as a dim 'star', at present in the constellation Capricornus. In 1781 the astronomer William Herschel looked at it through a telescope and saw a small disc instead of a point of light. He thought at first it was a comet, but its motion showed it was a planet, the first new planet to be discovered beyond Saturn.

## FACT FILE

### URANUS AND NEPTUNE DATA

| Planet | Uranus | Neptune |
|---|---|---|
| Distance from Sun (million km): | 2,870 | 4,497 |
| Year (Time to go round Sun): | 84.01 y | 164.8 y |
| Day (Time to revolve on axis): | 17 h 14 m | 16 h 7 m |
| Diameter at equator (km): | 51,118 | 50,538 |
| Known moons: | 17 | 8 |
| Mass (Earth=1): | 14.6 | 17.2 |
| Surface gravity (Earth=1): | 1.17 | 1.2 |

**Key**

1 Uranus
2 Miranda
3 Ariel
4 Umbriel
5 Titania
6 Oberon

← Orbit of Uranus around the Sun

**The moons of Uranus revolve almost at right angles to the direction of the planet's orbit around the Sun.**

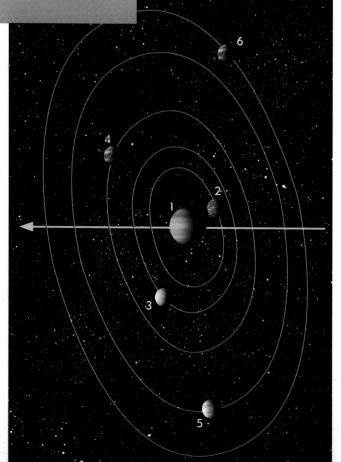

## Rolling around the Sun

Uranus seems to lie on its side – the axis around which it spins is tilted over by more than 90°. This means that each pole is in sunlight for half of the planet's 'year', while the other pole is in darkness.

Uranus is bluish-green with hardly any visible markings. Though it is smaller than Jupiter and Saturn, Uranus is still 64 times larger than Earth. It is mostly made up of hydrogen and helium, but its colour is due to clouds of methane crystals that float high in its atmosphere. Beneath these are clouds of ammonia, with frozen water further down. At the centre of the planet there may be a rocky core.

## The Blue Planet

Neptune is almost exactly the same size as Uranus, but more blue in colour. It is about 30 times as far from the Sun as the Earth is and takes just under 165 Earth years to go around the Sun. Not until the year 2011 will it have completed one orbit of the Sun since its discovery in September 1846. Neptune gets little more than a thousandth of the light and heat that we get from the Sun.

But Neptune is no colder than Uranus because heat flows from its interior. This flow of heat churns up the atmosphere and makes weather on Neptune more dynamic than it is on Uranus. Strong winds blow around the planet. When the *Voyager 2* spacecraft flew past Neptune in 1989 it saw a Great

A bright white cloud of methane crystals appears near the top of this false-colour image of Uranus.

High-altitude clouds float above the bluish methane haze of Neptune.

Dark Spot south of the equator. This was a storm 14,000 kilometres long – larger than the Earth. Elsewhere on the planet, other storms were going on. They included a disturbance topped by bright clouds, called the Scooter.

## HISTORY FILE

### NEPTUNE – THE PLANET FOUND ON PAPER

After its discovery in 1781, astronomers noticed that the speed at which Uranus orbits is irregular. Several astronomers had the idea that its movement was being disturbed by the gravitational pull of an unknown planet beyond it. Two young mathematicians, the Englishman John Couch Adams, and the Frenchman Urbain Leverrier, not knowing of each other's work, calculated where such a planet must be and its approximate mass. Their results were very similar, but it was using Leverrier's results that German astronomers found the new planet close to the position he had predicted. This was a triumph for the theory of gravitation, which was shown to work for the farthest planets.

# PLUTO AND BEYOND

**B**eyond Neptune the solar system is fringed by a belt of small, rocky objects. The largest of these, the planet Pluto, was discovered in 1930 and others began to be discovered in 1992. Astronomers believe there may be thousands of them.

Pluto is usually regarded as the outermost planet, but perhaps it should not be counted as a planet at all. It is smaller than some of the moons of the gas giants. It is made of a mixture of rock and ice as most of the satellites are. And it follows a strange orbit, strongly tilted compared to the orbits of the other planets, and strongly elliptical. At its farthest point it is 49 times as far from the Sun as the Earth is. But at its closest it comes closer to the Sun than Neptune does, though because of the tilt of its orbit, it is never close enough to Neptune to collide with it.

## The Double Planet

Pluto is so tiny and distant that detail on its surface cannot be made out by Earth-based telescopes. But Pluto has a satellite, Charon, whose diameter is 55 per cent of the diameter of Pluto, making the pair more like a double planet than an ordinary planet and satellite. Charon was discovered in 1978. Then astronomers had a piece of luck: from 1985 to 1990 Charon happened to pass repeatedly between the Earth and Pluto, something that won't happen again for 120 years. By studying the way the brightness of Pluto changed as Charon passed, astronomers could roughly map light and dark areas on Pluto's surface. They have also discovered that frozen methane and nitrogen cover its surface.

## HISTORY FILE

### THE WRONG PLANET IN THE RIGHT PLACE

Even after the discovery of Neptune, astronomers thought there were disturbances of Uranus that Neptune couldn't be responsible for. The astronomer Percival Lowell worked out the probable size, mass and orbit of 'Planet X', and spent years searching for it. In 1929, 13 years after Lowell's death, Clyde Tombaugh took up the search and found Pluto in January 1930. Its position and orbit were close to what Lowell had predicted, but Pluto is far too small to have affected Uranus noticeably. And anyway, there do not now seem to be any disturbances to the orbit of Uranus apart from those due to Neptune. Finding Pluto appears to have been a fluke.

**The distant Sun feebly lights up the dark, frozen surface of Pluto.**

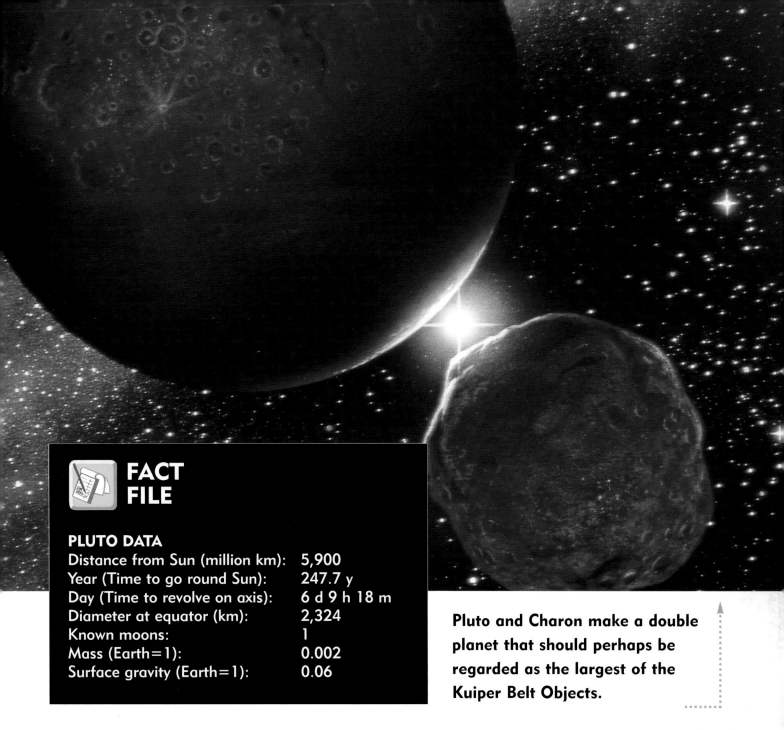

**PLUTO DATA**

| | |
|---|---|
| Distance from Sun (million km): | 5,900 |
| Year (Time to go round Sun): | 247.7 y |
| Day (Time to revolve on axis): | 6 d 9 h 18 m |
| Diameter at equator (km): | 2,324 |
| Known moons: | 1 |
| Mass (Earth=1): | 0.002 |
| Surface gravity (Earth=1): | 0.06 |

**Pluto and Charon make a double planet that should perhaps be regarded as the largest of the Kuiper Belt Objects.**

## The Kuiper Belt

For a long time, astronomers have searched for objects beyond Pluto. If there are any large objects, they are too far away to affect the known planets noticeably by their gravity. But around 1950 two astronomers, Kenneth Essex Edgeworth and Gerard Kuiper, independently suggested that some comets come from a belt of unseen objects circling the Sun at about the distance of Pluto, or farther. The first object in what is now called the Kuiper Belt was found in 1992. Within a few years, 60 of these KBOs (Kuiper Belt Objects) had been discovered. The largest was only 500 km across. Objects as small as this, or smaller, do not have strong enough gravity to

be pulled into a globe shape. About half of all known KBOs are trapped by Neptune's gravity, moving around the Sun in 1.5 times as long as it takes Neptune. Pluto does the same, so these KBOs are called 'Plutinos' ('little Plutos').

The KBOs are matter 'left over' from the birth of the solar system. If all of them (including the still undiscovered ones) were put together, they would probably make a single planet about the size of the Earth. Astronomers would like to find a 'Planet X', at least as large as Pluto, out beyond the known planets. This is still possible. But such a planet would have to be very faint and slow-moving to have been missed, and must be very far away indeed.

# PLANETARY MOONS

There are few natural satellites in the inner solar system. Mercury and Venus have none. The Earth has just one, the Moon. Mars has two tiny satellites, which are probably asteroids that were captured by the planet's gravity.

But things are very different in the outer solar system. The four gas giants are surrounded by their own small systems of orbiting moons. Jupiter has 16 satellites, Saturn 19, Uranus 17 and Neptune 8.

## Birth of the Satellites

Jupiter's moons demonstrate how planets came to have satellites. The eight innermost moons were created at the same time as the planet. They orbit above Jupiter's equator and move in the same direction that Jupiter rotates.

The next four satellites form a group, with a big gap between them and the inner moons. Their orbits are strongly tilted to Jupiter's equator. Far beyond these is another group of four, also strongly tilted and revolving around the planet the opposite way to all the rest. These two groups were probably formed from asteroids being broken up by impacts and 'captured' by Jupiter's gravity.

## Fire and Ice

Satellites can be very different from each other. Io, the innermost of the four largest moons of Jupiter, is

**The largest moons in the solar system are larger than the planet Pluto.**

highly volcanic. Its interior is heated as Io is stretched and squeezed by Jupiter's gravitational field, and the result is continuous spectacular volcanic eruptions of orange, white and black sulphur. These volcanoes are the hottest surface locations anywhere in the solar system apart from the Sun.

Another satellite of Jupiter, Europa, is covered

**The nine largest satellites of Saturn. Phoebe and Iapetus are so far away from Saturn that they have to be shown separately.**

**Key**
1 Saturn
2 Mimas
3 Enceladus
4 Tethys
5 Dione
6 Rhea
7 Titan
8 Hyperion
9 Iapetus
10 Phoebe

A sulphur volcano erupts on the horizon of Io, the volcanic satellite of Jupiter. Reddish sulphur compounds produced in past eruptions cover the surface.

with a smooth layer of ice, perhaps 100 kilometres thick. The satellite looks as smooth as a billiard ball. Beneath the ice there is probably liquid water, and it is possible that primitive life has developed there. Callisto – another of Jupiter's satellites – is also covered with ice but the surface is cratered and rough. Scientists believe there is salty water under the ice.

Saturn's largest moon, Titan, has a thick atmosphere, filled with a 'smog' of carbon compounds. Early in the twenty-first century the *Huygens* space probe will parachute into Titan's atmosphere to study the moon and see whether conditions exist like those on the Earth before life appeared – or even whether simple life has developed.

The most battered-looking satellite in the solar system is Miranda, a small moon of Uranus. The surface of Miranda is torn by huge valleys and ridges. Miranda seems to have been smashed by some impact in the past, with the pieces reassembling themselves afterwards.

 **FUTURE FILE**

### THE FATE OF THE MOONS
All satellites' orbits change over time. Our Moon is slowly spiralling away from the Earth. But Triton, the largest moon of Neptune, is slowly spiralling inwards towards the planet. In a billion years, Triton will probably break up to form a ring more spectacular than Saturn's.

# METEORS AND METEORITES

**W**atch the sky on a clear night, and several times in an hour you will see what seems to be a star darting across the night sky and disappearing. Sometimes it leaves a trail that glows briefly. This 'shooting star' or 'falling star' is caused by a grain of dust falling to Earth from space and burning up because of friction with the air. The scientific name for a shooting star is a **meteor** and the grain of dust that causes it is called a meteoroid.

## FACT FILE

### METEOR AND METEORITE DATA

★ Largest meteorite: fell in prehistoric times at Hoba West, near Grootfontein, Namibia; weight: 59 tonnes (meteorite still lies where it fell).

★ Heaviest meteor shower: the Leonids of 1966, which on 17 November reached a rate of 60,000 per hour for 40 minutes.

★ Best-preserved meteorite crater: Meteor Crater (also called Barringer Crater), Arizona, USA; 1.26 kilometres wide, 175 metres deep.

★ Mass of meteoroids entering atmosphere daily: approximately 1,000 tonnes.

★ Average speed of observed meteors: 40 kilometres per second.

**Pieces of rock are mixed with iron in this thin slice of a meteorite found in the Chilean desert.**

**Meteor Crater in Arizona was probably formed about 27,000 years ago.**

## Comet Dust

Meteor showers can be seen on certain dates every year. The number of meteors can briefly rise to hundreds or even thousands per hour at these times. Meteor showers occur when the Earth crosses a trail of dust left behind by a comet along its orbit – either a comet that still exists or one that has broken up. For example, two showers called the Eta Aquarids and the Orionids are seen on the two occasions in the year when the Earth crosses the dust trail of Halley's Comet.

Very occasionally, larger chunks of rock enter the atmosphere, which are so big that they are not completely burned away. The remaining piece of rock that falls to the ground is called a **meteorite**. People have been slightly injured by meteorites but no one is known to have been killed by one.

Meteorites seem to have come from asteroids that have been broken up by collisions. Most are stony, but some are metallic, made of iron and nickel.

## Meteorites from Mars

Some meteorites seem, from the minerals they are made of, to have come from Mars. They must have been blown off the planet either by huge volcanic eruptions or by the impact of asteroids or large meteorites on Mars. In 1997 there was excitement when scientists claimed to have found substances produced by simple life forms in such meteorites. But many scientists now think the substances were formed on Earth in other ways.

**A glowing meteor trail is left as a grain of interplanetary dust hurtles through the atmosphere and is burned up by friction.**

 **TEST FILE**

### MAJOR METEOR SHOWERS

A meteor shower builds up to a maximum over several days or even weeks, and then dies away again. Meteors can appear all over the sky, but if their paths are traced back, they seem to come from a single point, called the radiant of the shower.

The shower is named after the constellation in which the radiant lies. Meteor showers appear on the same dates each year.

| Date of Maximum | Name of Shower | Position of Radiant |
| --- | --- | --- |
| 3 January | Quadrantids | Boötes (there used to be a constellation here called The Quadrant) |
| 4 May | Eta Aquarids | Aquarius (near star Eta Aquarii) |
| 11 August | Perseids | Perseus |
| 20 October | Orionids | Orion |
| 16 November | Leonids | Leo |
| 13 December | Geminids | Gemini |

# COMETS

very few years a spectacular comet crosses the skies. It starts far from the Sun, a faint dot of light looking like a fuzzy star. But over a period of months, as it comes closer to the Sun, it grows a tail, or, more usually, two – one a misty, curved tail of dust, the other a straight tail of glowing gas. At its closest to the Sun, the comet may have tails stretching across millions of kilometres of space. When the comet has passed the Sun, its tails shorten and grow fainter, and finally disappear.

Most comets are seen only once. But some reappear, again and again, moving around elliptical orbits. Halley's Comet, the most famous comet of all, travels as close as 90 million kilometres to the Sun – 60 per cent of the Earth's distance. In the outermost part of its orbit, the comet travels out to 35 times the Earth's distance from the Sun – beyond the orbit of Neptune.

**Gas and dust stream from the nucleus of Halley's Comet, as photographed by the *Giotto* spacecraft.**

Some comets take much longer to revisit the inner solar system. One of the most spectacular comets of recent years was Hale-Bopp, which passed the Sun on 1 April 1998. By studying its movements, astronomers calculated that it had last passed Earth in 2214 BC. If it isn't disturbed by some object in the outer solar system, it will return in the year 6210.

**A comet's tail always points away from the Sun. It grows as it approaches the Sun and shrinks as it moves away.**

## FACT FILE

### WHEN HALLEY MET GIOTTO
Space probes from several nations flew close to Halley's Comet at its most recent appearance in 1986. The European Space Agency craft *Giotto* came closest. Some of its instruments were knocked out as the probe was blasted by a dust storm from the comet. Pictures from *Giotto* showed the nucleus was darker than coal.

**Key**
1  Tail lengthens as comet approaches Sun
2  Tail longest closest to Sun
3  Tail shrinks as comet moves away from Sun
→  Path of comet

# HISTORY FILE

## NOTABLE COMETS

★ Comets have collided with the Earth in the past. One fell over the Tunguska region of Siberia in 1908, devastating an area of forest 600 kilometres across. Fortunately the area was uninhabited.

★ Comet Encke has been seen scores of times, because it takes slightly less than 3 years and 4 months to go round the Sun. It comes closer to the Sun than Mercury's average distance.

★ People used to think that every comet was a completely new event. The seventeenth-century English astronomer Edmond Halley realized that a certain comet was reappearing every 76 years. Halley predicted that it would come again in 1758. It appeared on time, and was named after him.

★ The Great Comet of 1843 developed a tail that was 330 million kilometres long – more than twice the distance of the Earth from the Sun.

★ In 1910 there were prophecies that all life on Earth would be wiped out when the Earth passed through the tail of Halley's Comet. In fact, the event had no effect on Earth at all.

★ In June 1998 the *SOHO (Solar and Heliospheric Observatory)* robot space probe observed two comets crashing into the Sun. The tiny mass of the comets made no noticeable impact on the Sun.

## Anatomy of a Comet

The solid part of a comet is called the nucleus. The nucleus is a mixture of rock and 'ices'. Ices are not just frozen water, but can be frozen carbon dioxide, methane, or ammonia. There are two vast stores of millions of comet nuclei beyond the planets. One is the Kuiper Belt, just outside the orbit of Neptune; the other is the Oort Cloud, which forms a spherical shell around the solar system. From time to time, one of these 'sleeping comets' starts to fall inwards towards the Sun.

When a comet nucleus comes within the orbit of Jupiter, the warmth of the Sun causes some of the ice to turn into gas. Great fountains of gas and dust erupt from the nucleus. The gas spreads out around the nucleus in a huge globe, called the coma. The solar wind, a constant stream of subatomic particles (mostly protons and electrons) from the Sun, blows the gas and dust away from the comet nucleus to form the tails.

**Halley's comet reappears every 76 years and usually makes a spectacular sight.**

# EXPLORATION

Human beings have taken just a few small steps on the long journey of exploring the solar system. The first journey beyond Earth was a single orbit of the planet by the Russian cosmonaut Yuri Gagarin in 1961. In 1969 the first American astronauts travelled to the Moon. In six missions over the next 3½ years, 12 men walked on the Moon, studied its rocks and brought samples back to Earth.

## Crowded Orbits

Though human beings have not been back to the Moon since 1972, many have gone into orbit around Earth. Only Russia and the United States launch manned spacecraft, but they carry space travellers of many nationalities.

The neighbourhood of Earth has become more and more crowded. Thousands of satellites have been launched to survey the weather and climate, carry TV, radio and phone signals and computer data, spy on military secrets, study the planet's resources and view space from above our hazy, turbulent atmosphere.

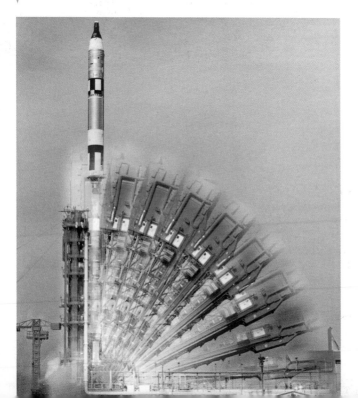

**This multiple-exposure picture shows a US *Titan II* rocket being raised into launch position and lifting off carrying a *Gemini* two-man capsule.**

**A *Voyager* space probe flying past Saturn.**

## Robot Explorers

Unmanned space probes have led the way across the solar system. They orbited the Moon and made crash landings before the first landing by astronauts. The first craft to fly by another planet was the American *Mariner 2* in 1962, flying past Venus. Later, Soviet probes parachuted down through the atmosphere of Venus and sent back photographs of the surface before the heat and pressure destroyed them.

In 1976 two American *Viking* craft landed on Mars and sent back pictures of the surface, and carried out chemical experiments to search for life in the soil. In 1997 they were followed by the *Pathfinder* mission, which carried a small robot rover.

## Space Odysseys

In the 1970s two *Pioneer* spacecraft and two *Voyager* craft were launched and carried out some of the greatest space journeys ever. Visiting Jupiter first, they used its huge gravity field to swing them on, gaining a speed boost that carried them on past the other outer planets. Between them the *Pioneer* and *Voyager* craft visited Saturn, Uranus and Neptune, leaving Pluto the only planet in the solar system that has not yet been visited. Now they will drift away from the region of the planets, until in hundreds of thousands of years they may reach other planetary systems.

# FACT FILE

## MILESTONES IN SPACE EXPLORATION

This table shows some important space missions. They are not necessarily the first of their kind, but they are the first really successful ones.

The *Hubble Space Telescope* is launched from the cargo bay of a Space Shuttle.

| Launch date | Craft | Mission Notes |
|---|---|---|
| 12 April 1961 | Vostok 1 | Yuri Gagarin, first human being in space, orbited the Earth. |
| 27 August 1962 | Mariner 2 | Flyby of Venus. |
| 16 July 1969 | Apollo 11 | First Moon landing. |
| 18 August 1970 | Venera 7 | Venus landing – transmitted for 23 minutes after landing. |
| 2 March 1972 | Pioneer 10 | Flew past Jupiter; followed a year later by *Pioneer 11*, which also flew by Saturn. |
| 3 November 1973 | Mariner 10 | Three encounters with Mercury, following Venus flyby. |
| 20 August 1975 | Viking 1 | Mission to Mars, with orbiter and lander; closely followed by *Viking 2*. Both landers transmitted data for years. |
| 5 September 1977 | Voyager 1 | Flew by Jupiter and Saturn. *Voyager 2* followed, and visited Jupiter, Saturn, Uranus and Neptune. |
| 12 April 1981 | Space Shuttle | First flight to Earth orbit of reusable spacecraft. |
| 2 July 1985 | Giotto | Close approach to nucleus of Halley's Comet. Japanese and Russian spacecraft also observed the comet. |
| 20 February 1986 | Mir | Soviet (now Russian) space station. Cosmonauts have set endurance records, some staying in space for over a year. |
| 18 October 1989 | Galileo | Probe parachuted into Jupiter's atmosphere; orbiter toured Jupiter's satellites. |
| 6 October 1990 | Ulysses | Flew by Jupiter and went on to fly over poles of Sun. |
| 4 December 1996 | Pathfinder | Explored a small area of Mars with *Sojourner Truth*, a mini-rover vehicle. |
| 15 October 1997 | Cassini | Probe to Saturn, due to arrive in 2004 and parachute *Huygens* probe into atmosphere of satellite Titan. |

The *Huygens* probe will parachute down through the smoggy atmosphere of Titan, Saturn's largest moon.

# MOON LANDINGS

etween 1969 and 1972 human beings explored a few small regions of the Moon. This US Moon programme, called Apollo, can be seen as a dress rehearsal for establishing settlements on the Moon and for journeys to the planets beyond.

Soviet robot craft led the way: *Luna 2* crashed on the Moon in 1959 and *Luna 9* made the first soft landing in 1966. Then human beings followed. *Apollo 8* was a 1968 test flight on which a crew of three flew around the Moon and back to Earth. At Christmas in the same year, *Apollo 10* went into orbit around the Moon. This time the lunar module – the part of the spacecraft designed to land on the Moon – separated from the command module. It descended to within 15 kilometres of the surface before rejoining the command module for the journey home.

## The Giant Leap

On 16 July 1969 *Apollo 11* took off on its way to the Moon, commanded by Neil Armstrong. On 20 July 1969 the lunar module *Eagle* touched down on a vast, rocky plain called the Sea of Tranquility. Watched by the world on TV, Armstrong crawled out

of the lunar module and spoke his famous line: "That's one small step for a man, one giant leap for mankind." He was followed by the lunar module pilot, Edwin 'Buzz' Aldrin. They gathered rocks and soil, set up several experiments and raised an American flag. Then they blasted off, rejoined the command module, which was orbiting the Moon, piloted by Michael Collins, and returned to Earth.

**The sequence of manoeuvres that took the Apollo astronauts to the Moon and back. To simplify the diagram, the Moon is shown in three positions along its orbit around the Earth.**

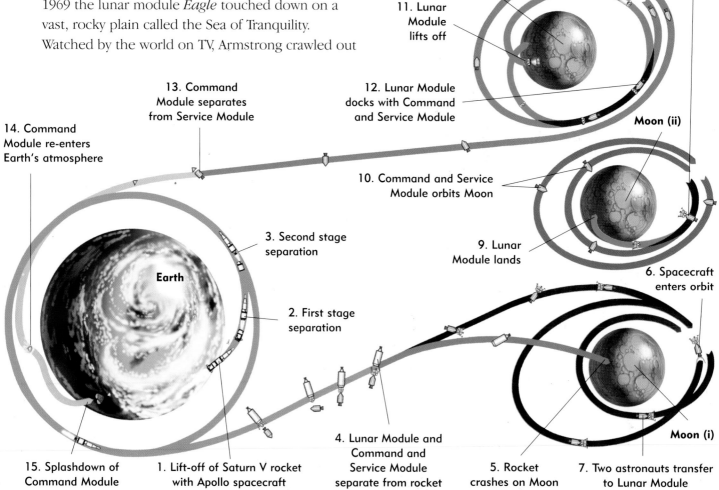

8. Lunar Module separates from the Command and Service Module

Moon (iii)

11. Lunar Module lifts off

13. Command Module separates from Service Module

12. Lunar Module docks with Command and Service Module

Moon (ii)

14. Command Module re-enters Earth's atmosphere

10. Command and Service Module orbits Moon

3. Second stage separation

Earth

9. Lunar Module lands

6. Spacecraft enters orbit

2. First stage separation

Moon (i)

4. Lunar Module and Command and Service Module separate from rocket

15. Splashdown of Command Module

1. Lift-off of Saturn V rocket with Apollo spacecraft

5. Rocket crashes on Moon

7. Two astronauts transfer to Lunar Module

**FACT FILE**

## APOLLO MISSION DATA
(Mission/Landing date/Landing site/
Mission notes)

★ *Apollo 11*
   20 July 1969
   Sea of Tranquillity
   First landing on the Moon by humans.

★ *Apollo 12*
   19 November 1969
   Ocean of Storms
   Landed near *Surveyor 3*, which had
      landed 2 years before.

★ *Apollo 13*
   (no landing)
   Oxygen tank exploded and power was
      reduced. Craft rounded Moon and
      returned, and crew were saved.

★ *Apollo 14*
   5 February 1971
   Crater Fra Mauro
   Astronauts used a handcart to carry
      equipment and rock samples.

★ *Apollo 15*
   30 July 1971
   Hadley Rille
   First use of a lunar rover vehicle.

★ *Apollo 16*
   20 April 1972
   Region near crater Descartes
   Mission commander carried out speed
      and turning trials of the lunar rover.

★ *Apollo 17*
   11 December 1972
   Near crater Littrow in Taurus mountains
   Longest Apollo mission, and the last.

An *Apollo 15* astronaut on the Moon.
On the right of the picture is the
lunar rover.

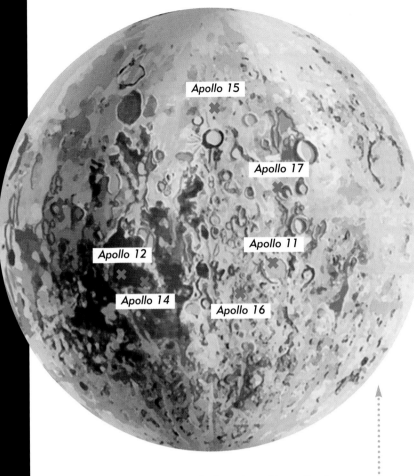

The landing sites of the Apollo missions.

### Later Missions

There were six more Apollo launches. *Apollo 13* was
a near-disaster when there was an onboard explosion.
The crippled craft could not land on the Moon, but it
had to fly around it before returning to Earth and
splashing down in the Pacific safely.

   The other missions were completely successful.
But there have been no more visitors to the surface
of the Moon since Eugene Cernan, commander of
the *Apollo 17* mission, climbed into his lunar module
in December 1972 and returned to Earth.

The *International Space Station*, the first colony in space, began to be assembled in orbit in November 1998.

The DC-XA is a planned US reusable spacecraft, designed to be lighter and cheaper than the Shuttle.

We are still busily exploring the solar system and robot probes are leading the way. The *Galileo* spacecraft, which arrived at Jupiter in 1995, is still wandering among the giant planet's satellites. The *Cassini/Huygens* expedition will vastly increase our knowledge of Saturn and its satellites during the 4-year mission planned for 2004, when it arrives at the planet. The *Pluto Kuiper Express* is expected to fly by Pluto, the last unvisited planet, in about 2011. Some day robot explorers may work successfully in the extreme heat and pressure on the surface of Venus.

The twenty-first century will see new telescopes in space. Giant radio observatories may be built on the far side of the Moon, where they will be shielded from the radio pollution of the Earth. The *Next Generation Space Telescope* – a more advanced version of today's *Hubble Space Telescope* – is planned to observe infra-red light – heat radiation – from the universe. It will be placed in an orbit somewhere beyond the Moon, so that it is not affected by the heat that radiates from the Earth.

In this artist's impression, the first explorers on Mars observe a sandstorm.

## Colonizing Space

As the twenty-first century progresses, human beings may spread through the solar system. The *International Space Station,* in orbit around the Earth, will probably grow larger. Space tourism might develop, with fare-paying travellers spending weekends in orbit and taking holidays on the Moon.

Huge space colonies may be built in orbit around the Earth. They will probably be built in the form of rotating wheels. People inside the rim of the wheel will be pressed to the outside, feeling a simulated force of gravity. This should avoid the problems of the weakening of bones and muscles that are caused by prolonged weightlessness.

## The Search For Life

Missions lasting many years may travel to Mars and then to the outer solar system. If they do, they will look for clues to the formation of the planets and the solar system in general. And they will search for traces of primitive life. Promising places to look are in liquid water beneath the ice that covers the surfaces of some satellites, or floats in the atmospheres of the giant planets.

 **FUTURE FILE**

### CROSSING THE SOLAR SYSTEM

Present-day journeys to the outer solar system take years, and new types of propulsion are needed. A slow, steady thrust continued for months or years could build up a large final speed. One possibility is nuclear energy; another is the 'light-yacht', which would have large sails and would be pushed along by the pressure of sunlight. A stronger thrust could be provided by atoms of antimatter, which are 'mirror-image' versions of ordinary atoms. When matter and antimatter collide, both vanish with the release of huge amounts of energy. If large amounts of antimatter could be made and safely stored, it could drive a spacecraft across the solar system at high speeds.

# DEATH OF THE SOLAR SYSTEM

For as long as the Sun lasts, the planets will circle it steadily, disturbed only by the occasional asteroid or comet impact. But far in the future, the solar system will die. The Sun has been shining for about 5 billion years, and there have been changes in its brightness during that time. It may become hotter during the next billion years, making life impossible on Earth.

But even if the Sun doesn't change during this time, it will run low on fuel in another 5 billion years, and will begin to burn helium instead. The change will prolong its life, but will certainly spell the end of life on Earth. The ageing Sun will swell to become a red giant star. It will become more than a hundred times as wide, swallowing Mercury and Venus, and filling the present orbit of the Earth.

These interstellar gas clouds have been disturbed by the shock wave from a supernova – a star that has exploded.

## FUTURE FILE

### THE END OF THE UNIVERSE

Astronomers think that long after the Sun has faded into darkness, other stars will be born from the gas clouds scattered through the Galaxy. But eventually the gas will be used up and starbirth will cease after a million million years. Yet the smallest, faintest stars may shine for 100 times longer than this. Much later, some of the dead stars will be swallowed into black holes growing at the heart of each galaxy, but most will escape from their galaxies and wander through space. The universe will have become a cold, dark place. No one knows whether life will evolve into a form that can survive into this distant future.

About 5 billion years from now, the Earth may be roasted by the swollen, dying Sun.

## Roasting the Earth

The Earth's orbit will expand as the Sun loses mass. Our planet may escape being swallowed up, but it will be roasted. The oceans and atmosphere will boil away and life on the planet will be impossible. Farther out in the solar system, the gas giants will shrink as their heated atmospheres escape into space. Life may evolve on newly warmed worlds like Saturn's satellite Titan or Jupiter's moon Europa. But these small bodies will not be able to keep their atmospheres, so life will be very short-lived there.

## The Fading of the Sun

After further millions of years the Sun will become a variable star, flaring and dimming erratically. Then, when the last of its fuel has been exhausted, it will fade and shrink until it is about the size of the Earth.

The Earth will become a cold cinder, incapable of supporting life. If human beings have mastered the art of travel to the stars that lie far away in space, they will already have escaped to the planets of some younger star, leaving the solar system behind them.

# GLOSSARY

**Asteroid** A minor planet, or planetoid. Most move around the Sun between Mars and Jupiter.

**Atmosphere** A layer of gases surrounding a planet or satellite.

**Comet** A small body consisting of a mixture of rock and ice orbiting the Sun.

**Constellations** Groups of stars seen from Earth.

**Day** The time the Earth takes to rotate once on its north-south axis. The word is also applied to the time that other planets and satellites take to rotate.

**Density** The mass of a substance in a given volume. It may be expressed as kilograms per cubic metre or in relation to the density of water.

**Elliptical** Shaped like an ellipse, a curve resembling a circle that is more or less flattened. The orbits of the planets and satellites are all elliptical.

**Light year** The distance that light travels in a year – 9.46 million million kilometres.

**Mass** The amount of matter in an object, measured in kilograms.

**Meteor** The phenomenon seen when a meteoroid falls into the Earth's atmosphere and is burned up by the heat generated by friction.

**Meteorite** A piece of rock sometimes found on the ground after the fall of a meteoroid.

**Meteoroid** A small piece of rock orbiting the Sun.

**Orbit** The path of an object around another body – such as a planet around the Sun. The orbits of nearly everything in the solar system are elliptical.

**Planet** An object consisting of rock and gas that revolves around a star.

**Pressure** A measure of the force that acts on a unit area of a substance.

**Radiation** Any energy that exists in the form of electromagnetic waves (such as light, X-rays, radio waves and microwaves) or streams of particles.

**Satellite** A small body, natural or artificial, revolving around a planet.

**Solar wind** A stream of electrically charged particles that blows outwards from the Sun.

**Star** A mass of gas in space, made hot by nuclear reactions.

**Year** The time that the Earth takes to travel around the Sun. The word is also applied to the time that other planets and satellites take to orbit the Sun.

# FURTHER INFO

## ORGANIZATIONS TO CONTACT

**Society for Popular Astronomy**
36 Fairway, Keyworth, Nottingham NG12 5DU
Web site: http://www.u-net.com/ph/spa
Caters for beginners in astronomy of all ages. The annual subscription includes four copies of the society's magazine 'Popular Astronomy', and at least six newsletters per year.

**The British Astronomical Association**
Burlington House, Piccadilly, London W1V 9AG
Tel: 0171 734 4145
Web site: http://www.ast.cam.ac.uk/~baa
Britain's senior astronomical society for serious amateurs was founded in 1890. There are special subscription rates for junior members (under 18).

## BOOKS TO READ

*New Guide to the Planets* by Patrick Moore (Sidgwick & Jackson, 1993)
*Marshall Children's Guide to Astronomy* edited by Jacqueline Mitton and Simon Mitton (Marshall Publishing, 1998)
*Our Solar System* by Jon Kirkwood (Watts, 1998)
*The Space Atlas* by Heather Couper and Nigel Henbest (Dorling Kindersley, 1992)

## WEB SITES

http://www.ast.cam.ac.uk
Page maintained by the University of Cambridge Institute of Astronomy and other astronomical organizations in Cambridge. It provides numerous links to sources of astronomical information.

http://www.nasa.gov
The home page of NASA. Vast quantities of information about the solar system and human exploration of space.

http://www.seds.org/billa/tnp
The Nine Planets: A Multimedia Tour of the Solar System. A site maintained by Bill Arnett, describing the history, mythology, and current scientific knowledge of each of the planets, moons and other objects in the solar system.

# INDEX